SPIDERS

A PORTRAIT OF THE ANIMAL WORLD

Paul Sterry

SMITHMARK

This edition published by SMITHMARK Publishers, a division of U. S. Media Holdings, Inc.,
16 East 32nd Street, New York, NY 10016

SMITHMARK books are available for bulk purchase for sales promotion and premium use.
For details write or call the manager of special sales,
SMITHMARK Publishers,
16 East 32nd Street, New York, NY 10016; (212) 532-6600.

This book was designed and produced by
Todtri Productions Limited
P.O. Box 572
New York, NY 10116-0572
Fax: (212) 279-1241

Printed and bound in Singapore

ISBN 0-7651-9968-8

Author: Paul Sterry

Publisher: Robert Tod
Book Designer: Mark Weinberg
Production Coordinator: Heather Weigel
Senior Editor: Edward Douglas
Project Editor: Cynthia Sternau
Assistant Editor: Linda Greer
DTP Associate: Michael Walther
Typesetting: Command-O, NYC

PHOTO CREDITS
Photographer/Page Number

Dembinsky Photo Associates
Ed Kanze 50
Gary Meszaros 28 (bottom), 39 (top)
Bill Lea 17 (bottom)
Skip Moody 4, 6, 43
Ted Nelson 19

Brian Kenney 5, 13, 15 (bottom), 18 (left & right), 21, 23 (top & bottom),
24-25, 27 (top & bottom), 30, 31, 32, 34, 36-37, 39 (bottom), 46, 48-49, 52 (top),
54 (bottom), 56, 57, 59 (top & bottom), 63 (bottom), 66, 67, 70, 71

Joe McDonald 41

Gail Shumway 62

Tom Stack & Associates
John Cancalosi 22, 47
Lysbeth Corsi 16 (top)
David M. Dennis 3, 35 (top), 53
George D. Dodge 12
Kerry T. Givens 40, 54 (top)
Rod Planck 7, 11 (bottom), 28 (top), 29, 33, 51 (bottom), 61 (bottom), 63 (top)
Milton Rand 15 (top), 42, 45, 55
John Shaw 26, 35 (bottom), 38, 52 (bottom)
Denise Tackett 17 (top)
G. & D. Thompson 10

The Wildlife Collection
Ken Deitcher 51 (top), 69
John Guiustina 8-9, 16 (bottom), 20
Clay Myers 58, 61 (top)
Tim Laman 11 (top), 14, 60, 64-65, 68

INTRODUCTION

Long legs and large fangs are typical of wolf spiders. A head-on view of this Florida wolf spider reveals its beady, paired eyes.

Love them or hate them, spiders are a fact of life for most people around the world. They are found on every continent and have representatives in almost every terrestrial habitat capable of supporting life. Some spiders have ventured into the world of fresh water and a few can even tolerate exposure to salt water. The fact that almost everyone can recognize a spider might be thought to imply uniformity among the group as a whole. This is far from the case, however, and there is huge variation in both color and size: Some species are smaller than a grain of rice, and the largest can exceed the span of a man's hand.

Spiders are also among the most numerous of invertebrate groups and are particularly abundant in grassland and woodland habitats. Given the overlap between these natural habitats and our own yards and gardens, it is not surprising that we come into contact with spiders on a regular basis. Add to this many spiders' predilection for dark nooks and crannies, and many species have become familiar companions at home, whether they are welcome or unwelcome visitors.

For the amateur naturalist, spiders offer a wealth of opportunities for observation and study. Their sharpened senses and awareness of the world can make observation a challenge, but most species are confident enough to allow a cautious approach. Some spiders are

beautifully marked and attractive simply to look at. In some species, the coloration may clearly serve as camouflage, but for others the reasons for striking colors may be difficult to explain, and are perhaps best just appreciated and enjoyed. For the careful observer, a more prolonged study will reveal fascinating and complex behavior patterns—in their own way just as rewarding as watching birds or mammals.

Aside from the eight legs which set them apart from other most superficially similar invertebrates, one of the most obvious and striking features of spiders is the ability to produce silk. For some species, this is used primarily in feeding, but for most spiders, webs and the silk from which they are made play an integral part in almost all aspects of their lives.

Another feature which all spiders have in common is that they are predators, for the most part specializing in the capture of other invertebrates. Their dexterity with their legs and the binding properties of silk are important, but it is their fangs and venom production that are the keys to their success. Not surprisingly, this armory of weapons is as much use in defense as it is in attack, and their normally aggressive tendencies must be modified during the delicate process of courtship and mating.

Man has always had a somewhat ambiguous relationship with spiders. As potent symbols of good luck to some and bad luck to others, these fascinating creatures feature heavily in both written legends and popular myths. Some people develop a deep-seated phobia to spiders, while others find them fascinating and keep them as pets. Few remain indifferent to the sight of a spider in the sink or a curtain of webs in a dark, damp cellar, and for some, spiders are the stuff of nightmares.

Compared to the rest of its body, the distended abdomen of the mabel orchard spider, Leucauge mabelae, *has a soft skin which is also brightly colored.*

Etched by dew drops, this spider web would otherwise be almost invisible to the eyes both of human onlookers—and potential prey animals such as flying insects.

WHAT IS A SPIDER?

Spiders find their place in the animal kingdom among the invertebrates—creatures without backbones, and the group to which nearly three-quarters of all animal species known to science belong. More than that, however, they belong to what is arguably the most important invertebrate phylum—that comprising the Arthropods. In common with other members of this group, which includes insects, crustaceans, millipedes, and centipedes, spiders are characterized by having jointed legs. Lacking an internal skeleton, they have instead an external one in the form of a hard outer casing.

Within the Arthropods, spiders belong to a further subdivision, or class, called the Arachnida; they have among their cousins scorpions, pseudoscorpions, whip scorpions, ticks, and mites. For the average person, however, the finer points of invertebrate classification are somewhat irrelevant. Most spiders are instantly recognizable for what they are; the eight legs and proportion of body size to leg length betray their identity.

Structure and Growth

The most widely known group of Arthropods to which spiders are superficially similar are the insects, and both have the same hardened exoskeleton and jointed legs. Insects have a body divided into three clearly segmented parts: the head, thorax, and the abdomen. Among spiders, however, the body is divided into only two well-defined sections, the head and thorax are fused to form a cephalothorax, also referred to as the prosoma. Covered by a hardened and protective carapace, this part of the body is connected to the sac-like abdomen by a narrow, waisted pedicel.

Situated at the front of the prosoma are the eyes, generally eight in number, which are vital to a spider's ability to interpret the world around it. The most important eyes are the median pair; these are surrounded by smaller eyes whose function may be to cope with vision at low light levels. Insects have eyes that comprise numerous separate cells, each with its own lens, known as compound eyes. By contrast, those of spiders are simple in terms of structure; there is a single lens focusing onto a layer of light-sensitive cells.

Despite the intimidating stare created by the eyes of many larger species, most spiders find their sense of touch equally important to

Following page: Poised on delicate legs, a northern black widow spider, **Latrodectus variolus***, is awaiting its next victim. This species, found in the eastern United States, often enters houses as an unwelcome guest.*

Jumping spiders of the family Salticidae are famed for their ability to leap great distances relative to their body size. This enables them both to escape danger and to capture prey.

Caught in the web of a black-and-white Argiope spider, the fate of this alfalfa butterfly is sealed.

many species resemble miniature legs. These can be used to assist in the manipulation of food, but in males are modified and important in mating.

Beneath the prosoma are attached the four pairs of legs which so readily allow spiders to be recognized by human beings. They are jointed in the same manner as those of insects, and the various sections have the same hardened cuticle as the rest of the spider's body. Were it not for the fact that, between the joints, the cuticle is soft and flexible, movement would be somewhat restricted. As it is, with all six joints in the leg operating at a slightly different angle, a great deal of freedom of movement is achieved, and the necessary muscles are attached to the inside walls. At the tip of the last leg segment, known as the tarsus, are claws, three of which are found in most web-building spiders (other species have only two).

The upper surface of the prosoma is protected by a hardened plate known as the carapace. The same degree of strengthening and hardening is not found in the cuticle of the abdomen, which is comparatively soft and allows for considerable expansion. The upper surface of the abdomen is often attractively colored, with markings sometimes hinting at the segmented ancestry of spiders. Towards the front of the abdomen on the under surface are openings both to the respiratory system and to the reproductive system. Internally, the abdomen harbors the vital organs of the digestive, circulatory, reproductive, and excretory systems; respiration is facilitated by book lungs. This is the only way the primitive mygalomorphs breathe, but in more advanced spiders, a tracheal system of tubes has developed along the lines of that seen in insects. At the tip of the abdomen are the spinnerets used in the production and deployment of silk.

The main problem with having a hard exoskeleton is that it restricts the ability to grow freely. Like insect larvae and nymphs, young spiders overcome this problem by periodically molting. As with insects, the onset of this process is marked by a cessation in feeding. The first stage in molting occurs when the sides of the prosoma split below the carapace. The process is encouraged by movements of the spider's body and rhyth-

their daily lives. Sensory hairs are usually present over the entire body, as are special structures known as slit organs. Both types of sense organs are linked to the nervous system whose brain is also found in the prosoma. They help the spider oriente itself in its environment and detect prey or potential danger.

The mouth is also situated at the front of the spider's prosoma. The most notable appendages here are the pair of chelicerae which carry the all-important fangs; the fangs oppose one another in most species except in the primitive mygalomorphs, whose fangs thrust downwards. Adjacent to the chelicerae are the pedipalps, which in

The rather tattered appearance of the giant nephila spider's web betrays the fact that numerous victims have become ensnared in its silk. The spider will continue to repair any damage to the web as best it can.

A coating of sensitive hairs covers the body of an orb-web spider, Epeira regi. The hairs enable it to detect the slightest vibration in its surroundings.

mic pumping, and the split continues down the sides of the abdomen. The spider eventually extricates its legs and pulls itself free. There is a degree of flexibility in the new cuticle which allows expansion in body size to occur, but the process often has to be repeated many times during its life before a spider can achieve its full size. Not surprisingly, the spider is extremely vulnerable during the process of molting. It is usually performed while suspended on a silken thread, and often under the cover of darkness.

Classification

The relationship between spiders and their Arthropod cousins has been discussed previously, spiders belonging to the class Arachnida and the order Araneae; this latter subdivision separates them from other arachnids, including scorpions, false scorpions, harvestmen, ticks, mites, whip scorpions, sun scorpions, and a few other minor groupings.

Spiders are an extremely diverse group in terms of appearance and the number of species; there are more than thirty thousand species known to science at present and many more yet to be described. With such a scope as this, it would be impossible to cover spider classification comprehensively in a book of this size. The brief survey of the range of spiders that follows will, however, provide a useful background to their taxonomy. For the purposes of this book, two suborders are considered; these comprise the majority of species including those most familiar to spider enthusiasts.

The banana spider is found in the Amazon rain forest in Peru. Its large size enables it to catch comparatively large prey such as katydids and cockroaches.

Suspended in its elegant web, a golden-silk spider or calico spider, Nephila clavipes, awaits the arrival of an unsuspecting prey such as a butterfly.

The sub-order Orthognatha contains spiders commonly referred to as mygalomorphs, many of which are large and hairy. They are considered to be a primitive group primarily because of the organization of the chelicerae and fangs, which are driven vertically downwards into the victim. Many mygalomorphs live in underground burrows; among these are the so-called bird-eating spiders (family Theraphosidae), trap-door spiders (families Ctenizidae and Barychelidae), funnel-web spiders (sub-family Macrothgelinae) and purse-web spiders (family Atypidae). The majority of species are found in warm climates.

The sub-order Labidognatha is a far larger group and contains almost all the remaining spider species, including those most familiar to observant naturalists. The arrangement of the chelicerae—such that the fangs can operate in an almost opposing fashion—is a shared feature of the group and one which separates them from the mygalomorphs. The Labidognatha, sometimes called the Araneomorpha, also have a tracheal system of internal tubes to assist respiration. The sub-order contains both non-web-building as well as web-building representatives. Non-

web-building species include crab spiders (family Thomisidae), wolf spiders (family Lycosidae), and jumping spiders (family Salticidae). Web-builders include money spiders (family Linyphiidae), orb-web spiders (family Araneidae), daddy-long-legs spiders (family Pholcidae), widow spiders (family Theridiidae), and other funnel-web spiders (family Agelenidae).

A grass spider has just caught a hapless fly in its web. Venom injected through the fangs will kill the victim and soon begin to digest its body contents.

This Usambara orange baboon spider is sitting next to its shed skin. The old covering to the carapace can be seen clearly lying separated from the rest of the skin; this was the first part to become detached during the process of molting.

Like other arthropods, spiders periodically have to shed their skins in order to grow. Depending on the species, this may happen up to ten times in the life of an individual spider.

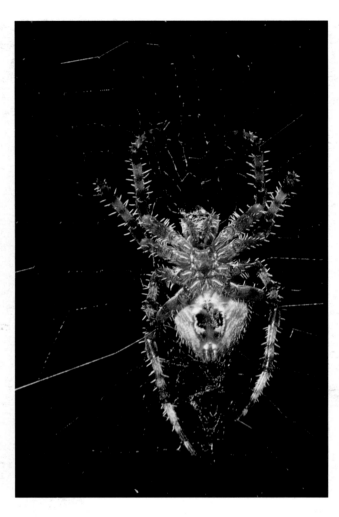

The four pairs of legs which characterize spiders can clearly be seen here, in addition to the spinnerets situated near the tip of the abdomen which are responsible for the production of silk.

Within the Labidognatha, experts recognize two groups, one of which contains spiders that possess a structure known as a cribellum, which enables extremely fine silk to be produced. Only a relatively small number of spider families belong to this group; the majority lack a cribellum.

Silk Production and Web-Building

Although the production of silk is by no means unique to spiders, this fascinating group of invertebrates has refined the uses to which it is put—to the point where spiders can be said to have made web construction their trademark.

Silk is a protein which is produced by glands of several different sorts situated in the abdomen. These open through pores or spigots on the spinnerets at the tip of the abdomen. Silk is secreted in liquid form but hardens as it is stretched, not by drying in the air; the protein fibers become oriented in the same direction by this process. Different glands produce silk with differing properties, each suited to a range of purposes. All spiders produce silk which serves as a lifeline when moving through the environment, as well as

Caught in the evening sunlight, the glistening silk strands of this golden-silk spider's web show how the species got its name.

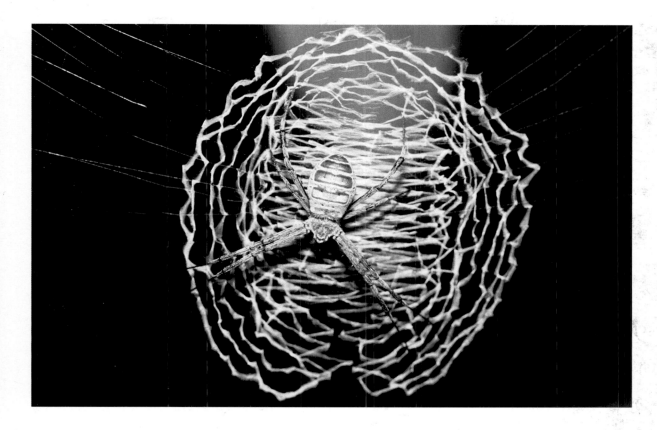

Not content with allowing the silk web to trap its victim, a St. Andrew's cross spider from Malaysia is poised to attack anything that strays into the strands.

Few people can appreciate the sheer numbers of spiders that thrive in open meadows until a happy combination of heavy dew and a low angle of sunlight combine to highlight their webs.

silk suitable for wrapping up prey and for the egg sac. Orb-web spiders produce other types of silk which assist in the construction and coating of their webs.

Sit in a meadow on a warm summer's day and you are likely to notice gossamer strands of silk festooning the vegetation and blowing in the breeze; it is most noticeable when backlit by bright sunlight. Although the origin of most of these silk threads will be tiny young spiders, these are not failed attempts at web-building. Rather, the spiderlings are using silk to assist their dispersal into the big, wide world. Watch closely and you may see the tiny spiders making their way to the tops of grass stems and other vegetation. With abdomens tilted towards the sky above, they release a stream of silk threads which are carried by updrafts of warm air. For a while, the weight of the spiderling, although small, is too great for the silk, but when enough has been produced the lift is great enough to carry them into the air. Now at the mercy of the wind, some are carried far away and travel many thousands of feet into the air.

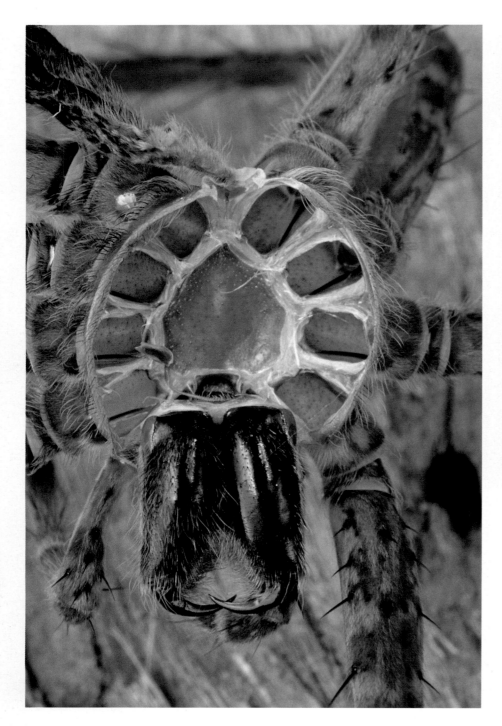

Spiders such as this black widow, **Latrodectus mactans,** *not only use silk to construct webs for catching prey and rearing young but also as a lifeline when moving around.*

Not all spider webs are constructed in a vertical plane. This one has undergone an attractive and seemingly perfect geometrical contortion.

PREDATORS!

It is remarkable that with a group so large and diverse as spiders, every member is carnivorous in its feeding habits. The majority feed on invertebrates, with insects featuring heavily in their diet. With the tremendous variation both in size and in form found among spiders, it is not surprising that a wide range of different prey animals is taken among specialist feeders. Some capture armored wood-lice, while a few species feed on other spiders or steal prey from other spiders' webs. Among the huge mygalomorph spiders in particular, there are some which regularly catch vertebrate prey, including small mammals and birds. A very few, such as the raft spider, have even perfected the art of fishing and can lure water creatures to their doom.

Fangs and Venom

When it comes to capturing and subduing prey, a spider's fangs and venom are its most important assets. As mentioned previously, the fangs are located on the chelicerae situated on either side of the mouth. In the often large but comparatively primitive mygalomorph spiders, the fangs are plunged into the victim with a downward stroke of the chelicerae. This action works perfectly well when the victim is on the ground and has the ground beneath it to counteract the force of the fangs. Without anything to press against, this system would be relatively inefficient when attempting to bite active prey off the ground. Other spiders, including all those that make orb-webs, have fangs which operate in a somewhat side-to-side manner, where the prey is punctured in a pincer-like movement.

Acting in the manner of hypodermic needles, fangs are hollow tubes through which venom passes as it is injected into the victim; the venom is produced by glands at the base of the fangs. The constituents and properties of venom vary from species to species, but in each case it serves the same initial purpose—namely to paralyze the victim. In some spiders, venom will kill the prey and at least partially digest the internal organs by the action of enzymes.

A large bird-eating spider, known as a mygalomorph, wanders over the forest floor of the Amazon rain forest. It can tackle prey the size of katydids, mice, and even small birds, if it can catch them.

Its size gives this Usambara baboon spider the confidence to wander at leisure over the forest floor. Few predators will tackle this large, African species.

Although spiders catch a variety of prey, they all, in effect, consume a liquid diet. Those species that inject enzymes into the victim with venom simply suck out the digested body contents, leaving behind an empty arthropod exoskeleton. Others macerate their prey with their mouthparts and regurgitate digestive enzymes onto the crushed victim; they later suck up the nutritious soup. The ingestion of body fluids is effected by a powerful sucking stomach situated towards the front of the digestive system.

Fangs and venom are useful not only in attack but also in self-defense. For anyone unfortunate enough to have felt the bite of a large house spider, perhaps when mishandling this species from a bathtub or sink, the sharp pain of the puncture wound is like a mild wasp sting, often exacerbated by the injection of venom. Although no lasting harm can be done by the bite of a house spider, the same cannot be said for a few other species. The Sydney funnel-web spider, *Atrax robustus*, is a notorious example whose bite can be lethal. On occasion it can be aggressive, especially when gardeners unintentionally disturb the female's funnel web in the soil. The other well-known example is the black widow, *Latrodectus mactans*, which is widespread in the United States. Although not often fatal, its bite causes severe pain which can last for more than a week.

Following page:
A true monster, this king baboon spider, Citharischius crawshayi, *lumbers over the African forest floor. With legs outstretched, it is the size of a man's palm.*

A familiar denizen of American houses, this house spider has made its rather untidy funnel-shaped web in a forgotten crevice. These creatures perform a valuable function in eating household insects.

Unaware of its peril, a resting damselfly is in imminent danger of being captured by a green lynx spider, Peucetia viridans. *The damselfly's ability to fly will be no match for the spider's speed.*

The bird-eating spider, Avicularia metallica, *comes from the tropical rain forests of Peru. Its large size has enabled it to capture a katydid, a sizable insect in its own right.*

The World of the Crab Spider

Picture a sunny summer day in a North American woodland clearing. Colorful wildflowers abound and are constantly visited by the nectar-feeding insects filling the air. One flower in particular looks especially inviting and attracts the attention of a passing fritillary butterfly. Lured by the prospect of sugar-rich nectar, the unsuspecting insect gets more than it bargained for: A perfectly camouflaged crab spider grabs it in a deadly embrace. For about half an hour, the butterfly and spider remain locked together, the butterfly seemingly indulging in an unrivaled meal. But, of course, it is the spider which is feasting, and when it finishes its meal, the intact but drained remains of the butterfly flutter in the wind and fall lifeless to the ground.

Seemingly, wherever in the world there are colorful flowers, there are crab spiders. Although not every species uses this form of deception, a great many crab spiders do, and some exhibit the most remarkable camouflage. Pink spiders sit on pink flowers and yellow spiders on yellow ones; some even show a remarkable similarity in terms of shape to the petals on which they are found.

A crab spider known as *Misumena vatia* is a commonly encountered species in Europe. It is

This attractive looking crab spider with a phantom cranefly as its victim is not a floral arrangement.

Perched on the white ray florets of a daisy, a crab spider appears invisible to the damselfly that decided to rest there.

Caught in a deadly embrace! This crab spider, Misumena vatia, *has caught a fritillary butterfly. When the victim has finally been drained of its body fluids, the dry skin of the insect will be discarded.*

A master of disguise, a crab spider has found the perfect flower to match its body color. It will lie in wait patiently for an insect to come and feed on the flower.

The fact that this crab spider has been able to subdue a hoverfly more than twice its own size testifies to the potency of its venom.

The process of paralyzing its victim may be swift, but to drain this hoverfly of its body fluids will take a crab spider up to an hour or so.

creamy yellow in color and generally favors yellow flowers on which to settle. It is also fond of gracing the flowers of ox-eye daisies, which are yellow in the center with an array of white ray florets spreading out from the middle. On these daisies, the spider invariably sits at the center, making the best use of its coloring.

Generally speaking, crab spiders grasp the flower on which they are sitting with the two hindmost pairs of legs, leaving the long front two pairs—which are armed with spines—pointing skywards in anticipation of a victim. When a butterfly or other insect settles on the flower to feed, the legs clamp shut and grab the victim; the internal contents are then drained. If the butterfly happens to land too far away on the flower to be caught, the spider will slowly and carefully shift its position to a more favorable one for capturing its prey.

Like others of its kind, this huntsman or giant crab spider, **Heteropoda venatoria,** *has a particularly flattened body and long, forward-angled legs; these features are typical of the family Sparassidae.*

Examine a spider's shed skin, such as this giant crab spider, **Heteropoda venatoria,** *and many arachnid features can easily be seen. Note the thin areas of skin which covered the paired eyes; in a living animal the eyes would be dark.*

Active Hunters

Instead of waiting for prey to come to them, some spiders adopt a much more active approach to feeding. Among the most conspicuous of these are the wolf spiders, which belong to the family Lycosidae. Species of the genera *Lycosa* and *Pardosa* are a common sight among leaf litter in woodlands around the world, especially in North America and Europe. They are most active on warm, sunny days and are often present in sufficient numbers to make the woodland floor appear to be almost seething. Wolf spiders are active predators whose main hunting sense is vision. Having spotted a potential victim a short distance away, they rush at their prey before it has time to effect an escape either by running or flying.

Wolf spiders are not the only group for whom vision is an important sense. Seen in close-up, the most striking features of the jumping spiders (family Salticidae) are their eyes which, in spider terms, are huge by comparison with the size of the head. Jumping spiders are incredibly alert to movements around them, whether these are from poten-

tial prey animals or stealthy observers. As their name suggests, species such as the commonly encountered zebra spider, *Salticus scenicus*, are able to perform leaps of more than thirty times their body length. Widespread in Europe, this species is often seen on garden walls and the sides of buildings. Like other jumping spiders it stalks its prey, including small insects and other spiders, until the point where it judges the distances between them are appropriate. The zebra spider then pounces on its prey, sometimes performing this feat on near-vertical surfaces. This critical jump is not undertaken, however, before the spider has secured itself with a silken safety line.

Not all active, predatory spiders use vision as their main hunting sense; some use their acute sense of touch in a manner analogous to web-building species. Raft spiders—*Dolomedes sp*, for example—are large creatures which, despite their size, are able to walk on the surface of water. A classic way of feeding for a raft spider is to lie in wait at the water's edge with just the two front legs touching the surface. Ripples caused by a small fish nibbling at surface debris or a dam-

Defying anything to enter its domain, a burrowing wolf spider is showing its large fangs and beady eyes which, in spider terms, are comparatively large.

Relying on its keen eyesight and turn of speed, this neotropical wolf spider from Guatemala has been able to catch a butterfly which foolishly visited the forest floor to drink.

selfly trapped in the surface film are enough to turn the raft spider into hunting mode. If an insect has fallen into the water, the spider quickly rushes across the water and paralyzes its prey with a bite from its not inconsiderable fangs. If the prey is a small fish, the spider will plunge through the water, grab the hapless creature with its legs, and quickly immobilize it.

Even more extraordinary is the water spider, a remarkable species which lives in lakes and ponds in Europe. Quiet observers sitting by the water's edge may occasionally see its silvery body moving through the water; the mirror-like effect is created by its air supply, trapped by hairs on its abdomen. It is only when observed in water or in a tank that its lifestyle and feeding habits can be truly appreciated.

Over a period of a day or so, this spider builds a domed underwater web—resembling an inverted bowl—among water plants. Having completed its task, the spider then makes repeated visits to the surface, where it replenishes its air supply by thrusting the tip of its abdomen through the surface film. Air is then transported into the underwater web tent and freed into the dome-shaped web. In its own spider-fashioned diving bell, the spider settles down to wait. Prey may include passing aquatic insects or distressed insects which have fallen into the water; silken strands connect the air-filled web to plants at or near the surface and vibrations are quickly picked up by the spider. Having captured its prey, the spider returns to the underwater lair to consume its meal in the manner of all other spiders.

One pair of extremely large eyes are characteristic of jumping spiders such as **Phidippus audax.** *The proportions of legs to body are also very different from those of other spider families.*

The reaction time of a fly was no match for the speed of the jumping spider, Phidippus arizonensis, *which stealthily crept close enough to be able to leap on its prey.*

Following page: The proportions of leg to body sizes are quite characteristic for wolf spiders, which belong to the family Lycosidae. These alert, active hunters rely on speed rather than a silk web to catch their prey.

A broad span of legs and a water-repellent skin coating enable the six-spotted fishing spider to walk on the surface of the water. When an insect becomes trapped in the surface film, the spider can detect ripples caused by its distress.

Living up to its name, a six-spotted fishing spider, Dolomedes triton, has just caught a minnow which was unfortunate enough to venture near the water surface.

When danger threatens, the fishing spider can dive underwater. Its presence there is often betrayed by the silvery effect caused by air trapped among its body hairs.

Taking advantage of a fallen, floating flower, a six-spotted fishing spider is still very much aware of any vibrations in the surface film caused by drowning insects.

Silken Traps

Although most spiders are famous for their webs, a few species use silk in unexpected but equally ingenious ways. The purse-web spider *Atypus affinis* lives inside a sealed silken tube, part of which is buried in the ground and the remainder of which lies on the ground like the finger of a glove. For most of the time, the spider remains in its underground retreat, but if vibrations tell it that an insect is walking over the exposed surface of the tube, it moves towards the source of the disturbance. Here, being a mygalomorph spider with downward-plunging fangs might appear to be a problem. The purse-web spider, however, walks upside down along the upper, inner surface of the silk tube. When it reaches the potential victim, its legs grab the insect through the tube and its huge fangs are thrust upwards into the victim. The prey is subsequently pulled through the silk, and the damaged area is repaired by the spider after it has fed.

Trap-door spiders also live in underground silken tubes although, as their English name suggests, a trapdoor can shut them off from the outside world. After dark, many species hold the door slightly ajar and rush out to grab passing prey.

One of the most remarkable uses of silk for catching prey is seen in the spitting spider, *Scytodes thoracica*, which is widespread in Europe and North America. The spider gingerly approaches its prey, which might be a fly or some other active insect. When close enough, it lifts up its prosoma and squirts a jet of silk from each of its fangs. A zig-zag pattern is created by side-to-side movements of the fangs, and the silk pins the victim to the surface on which it is resting. Venomous bites then subdue and kill the prey.

Equally bizarre are the habits of the bolas spiders, *Mastophora spp*, which are found throughout the Americas. After dark, the spider attaches a sticky blob of gum to a long

Alerted by vibrations caused by the grasshopper's legs, a grass spider creeps towards its victim, where a swift injection of venom will soon immobilize it.

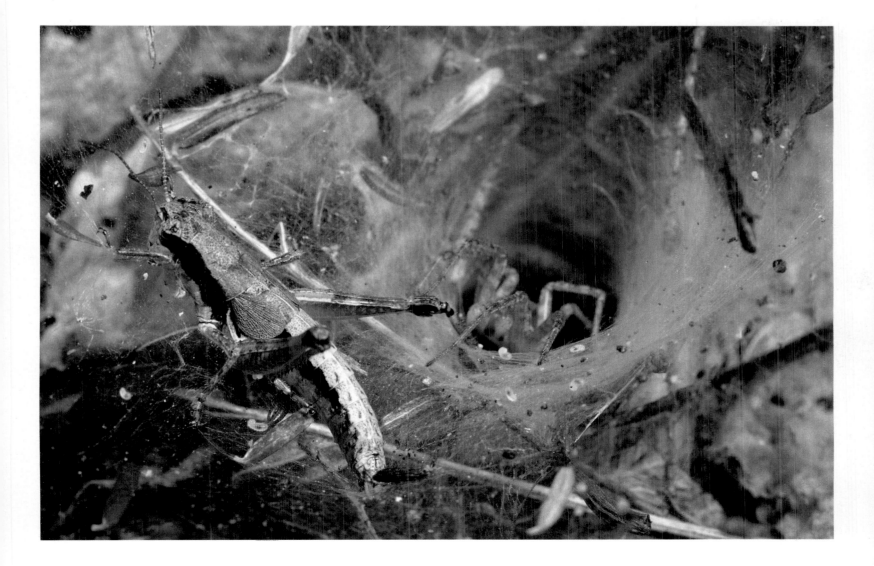

A grass spider
has just caught
a fly and is about
to retreat to the
safety of the silken
tube spun at the
center of its funnel-
shaped web.

silken thread and lies in wait beneath a leaf or branch. When a moth comes into range, the spider swings the viscid weight at the flying insect with a considerable degree of accuracy. The moth sticks to the gum, and is then retrieved by the spider and eaten.

Orb-Webs

Among the web-building spiders, it is those that construct the familiar orb-webs for which we reserve most of our admiration. Rightly so, for these are marvels of construc-

tion for such comparatively small creatures. It is often not until a frosty or dew-laden morning that these webs can be fully appreciated, at which time the sheer numbers of spiders in any given habitat will also cause some amazement.

Orb-web spiders belonging to the family Araneidae spin webs which, by and large, hang vertically and are designed to trap flying insects. Among larger, tropical spiders, the webs are sometimes sufficiently large and strong to catch small birds or bats, but

*Attractively outlined in dew, this grass spider's funnel-shaped web
will be of comparatively little use in catching prey until it has dried off.*

it is generally insects for which they are designed. Construction of the web invariably begins with the spider releasing a thin thread of silk from a secure and elevated piece of vegetation. The wind drifts the thread until it comes into contact with another branch or leaf. Having bridged this gap, the spider then lays a more substantial silk thread by crawling along the initial thread, which then becomes the uppermost horizontal thread in the web. A Y shape is then formed connecting the two upper attachment points to a twig or branch below; the center of the Y then forms the center of the web. The spider continues to create the outer silken framework of the web and then constructs the silken radiating lines. The next stage is to spin a spiral framework starting from the center and working outward. This done, the spider then starts to lay down sticky silk for the first time and retraces its steps inward, removing and eating the first spiral framework as it progresses.

With the web complete, the spider sits and waits for a meal to arrive; in some species, the shelter of a nearby leaf is employed, while other species sit upside down in the center of the web. When a flying insect hits the web and is ensnared, the vibrations caused by its distress alert the spider, which then rushes to its victim. Depending on the spider species involved, the insect will either be paralyzed on the spot or shrouded in more silk to subdue it before this happens. Spiders are able to cross their own sticky webs with impunity mainly because they grasp the non-sticky radial silk strands. A coating on the legs also acts as a non-stick "skin."

On a misty morning, the hammock webs of Linyphiid spiders can be equally impressive in terms of quantity, if not quality. Although the spiders themselves are generally small and do not produce the architectural marvels of their orb-web cousins, they create extensive sheets of silken webs which cover the vegetation by late summer. In some species, the sheet webs sag, giving the impression of a hammock. The spider lives beneath the web and detects the movement of any insect that drops onto the upper surface. It is then pulled through the web and paralyzed, and the damage caused to the web is repaired after the prey has been eaten.

Although not unique in their ability to produce silk, spiders have refined its use in the creation of webs to the point where no other animal group can compete in terms of skill and precision.

*This unlucky bush-cricket took a leap in the wrong direction and ended up in the web of a black-and-yellow Argiope spider, **Argiope aurantia**. The spider has paralyzed its victim and wrapped it in a silken cocoon for later consumption.*

SPIDER BEHAVIOR

For any predator whose main instinct is to kill and eat creatures of a similar size or smaller than itself, the processes of courtship and mating are liable to be fraught with danger. So it is with spiders, and many have evolved complex and fascinating ways of ensuring that a new generation is created without one member of a courting couple, invariably the male, becoming a meal for the other partner before successful fertilization has taken place.

Sex Differences

One of the most striking features of many spider species is the male's small size in relation to that of the female. An obvious explanation for the female's larger size is that she has to be able to produce large numbers of eggs—which in themselves occupy a large volume in relation to her own body size. Seen from another viewpoint, however, it is possible that, in some species at least, the male's size may be a positive advantage if he is too small for a female to consider as a meal.

The structure of the male and female reproductive apparatus and the means by which fertilization takes place require an intimate contact and one which, in most species, brings both parties into close contact with one another's fangs and mouthparts. Before mating can take place, the male has to go through a complicated procedure, transferring sperm from the genital opening to specially modified mouthparts. In most species, the male spider first spins a small web onto which he deposits sperm. Turning around, he now takes up the sperm into inflatable, bulblike storage organs called cymbiums, one of which is found near the tip of both palps. The cymbium acts in the manner of a syringe.

The female genital opening is called the epigyne, and it is into this that the male inserts the cymbium and transfers sperm; the shape of the epigyne exactly suits the shape of the male cymbium in each species. The female then stores the sperm in a special spermatophore and, in some species, it can be held for more than a year before being used to fertilize the eggs.

Courtship and Mating

Although in a few species where male and female spiders are of a similar size a rough-and-tumble approach to courtship is adopted, this strategy would spell certain doom for the male where the size difference between

Although some spiders simply suck their prey dry, species with powerful mouthparts sometimes chew the victim to speed up the process.

the sexes is dramatic. Not surprisingly, therefore, males take few chances, and go to great lengths to announce their arrival and induce a state of compliance in the female.

It is thought likely that, in many cases, the female is located by the male as a result of pheromones—attractant chemicals—that she releases. Among web-building species, the initial approach of the male involves tentative tugging on outer strands of the female's silken web. At first this usually invokes an attack response akin to having caught an insect in her web. Her response may necessitate a speedy retreat by the male but, undeterred, he will return again and again until she accepts that he is a potential partner rather than a meal.

Ground-dwelling spiders often make use of their legs when engaged in courtship. Among long-legged species it is common for the male

The thoughtful mother of this black-and-yellow mud-dauber wasp larva has provided it with a living food larder. Although immobilized by the wasp's sting, the spiders remain alive until eaten by the grub.

Following page: The baby spiders having emerged from their egg sac, this mother Carolina wolf spider, Lycosa carolinensis, now conveys her spiderlings,which scurry over her back.

This shamrock spider, Araneus trifolium, has just caught a wasp. The paralyzed victim is shrouded with silk to help subdue an otherwise potentially dangerous insect.

In common with other members of the genus, the spiny orb-weaver, Gasteracantha elipsoides, shows strange protrusions on its abdomen.

Sitting at the center of its web, a female orb-web spider has an abdomen which is full of developing eggs.

As the young spider-
lings grow, they
become more adventur-
ous. These baby green
lynx spiders are explor-
ing the silken world
of their nest web.

With her egg sac
grasped firmly in
her jaws, this female
nursery-web spider,
Pisaurina mira, is a
most attentive mother.
She will carry the egg
sac around until the
spiderlings hatch.

to stroke and tap the front legs of the female with his own front legs. After varying periods of time, the male then judges that a closer approach prior to mating is safe. Among jumping spiders and some wolf spiders—which are endowed with excellent vision in spider terms—the front legs are used in intriguing bouts of semaphore, and the tips of the legs are often brightly colored for this purposes.

Once having acquired the female's acceptance—or at least tolerance—the male can proceed with mating. In some species, this may involve the male facing the female in order to insert his palps into the epigyne. Alternatively, in some species the male is more circumspect in his approach and climbs over the top of her abdomen. The actual process of mating may take from one to several hours, depending on the species. When completed, the male again becomes vulnerable to attack and usually beats a hasty retreat unless the female is too quick for him.

Eggs and Egg-Laying

It has been argued, and not without some justification, that silk was first used by spiders in connection with egg-laying long before the first webs were constructed for catching prey. Evidence for this theory comes from the fact that even primitive, non-web-building spiders use silk in this way. Whatever its origins, the use of silk in the reproductive cycles of spiders continues to this day.

Prior to egg-laying in most species, the female spider spins a silken pad onto which the soft eggs and sperm are deposited. She then spins more silk and encloses the package in an egg cocoon; during this process the eggs are fertilized and their shells harden. The number of eggs laid in each batch varies from species to species, but between twenty and one hundred are commonly produced; some spiders, however, can lay more than one thousand eggs in a single batch. Each female is likely to lay several batches of eggs in her lifetime.

Although a few spiders abandon their eggs at this time, most show a degree of parental care, or at least concern, for their well-being. This often involves the female spinning a special web which surrounds and protects both the egg sac and the young spiderlings when they hatch. Other species, such as the wolf spiders, carry the

Seemingly unencumbered, this female wolf spider is carrying her egg sac attached firmly to the spinnerets at the tip of her abdomen.

Newly-hatched orb-web spiderlings huddle together for protection within the confines of the nest web woven by their mother.

egg sac around with them. With some spiders, it is attached to the spinnerets at the tip of the abdomen, while others grasp the sac with the jaws and at least one pair of legs.

When the young spiderlings hatch, using a special egg tooth to escape from the shell, they generally remain inside their egg sac until the first molt has been completed. Thereafter, those species for which a web has been constructed usually remain on or around the web, gaining nutrition at first from yolk inside their bodies, but subsequently from the female. In some spiders, the female is destined to die as a result of her labors and the young spiderlings feast on her body.

Walk through any woodland in Europe or North America and there are likely to be wolf spiders among the leaf litter. Some females will be carrying egg sacs, while others may appear to have rather knobby abdomens. On closer examination the female spider will be found to be covered with young spiderlings. Having hatched from the egg sac she so lovingly carried around with her, they clamber onto her back and are transported, protected, and fed until able to fend for themselves.

Photographed on a colorful flower in Costa Rica, a female green lynx spider is guarding her egg sac. She will continue her vigil until the baby spiderlings have hatched and are old enough to fend for themselves.

Protected by a hardened silken case and surrounded by a network of silken strands, the eggs of this argiope spider, Argiope trifasciata, will develop safe and sound.

Self-Defense

All spiders are predatory in their habits and, for their size, they are fearless hunters armed with powerful jaws, fangs, venom, and silk. Since the weapons of attack can also serve in defense, it might be supposed that they are invulnerable to attack. This is, however, far from the case. With bodies full of nutritious proteins and fats, spiders are very definitely on the menu for a host of other predators and parasites. In order to combat these depredations, spiders have evolved a variety of means of defending themselves—or avoiding being detected in the first place.

Threats and Dangers

Simple observation and mathematics will tell the naturalist that, with numbers of common house and garden spiders seeming not to vary from year to year, but with each female producing hundreds of offspring, the mortality rate for young spiders must be catastrophic. Birds, in particular, are especially significant predators judging by the numbers of spiders that are taken to feed the mouths of hungry chicks. Throughout the world, examples of spider predators can be found among almost every predatory animal group, including insects, centipedes, scorpions, reptiles,

One bite from the neotropical orb-weaver's venomous fangs means certain death for its froghopper prey.

As if its size alone were not enough to deter would-be predators, this king baboon spider has another trick up its sleeve—it raises its legs in a threat display and will shed irritating hairs in its attacker's face.

and amphibians. Even mammals will take a few spiders; members of the mygalomorphs with their large, juicy bodies are particularly succulent offerings for foraging creatures.

Death is not necessarily instantaneous for spiders, and for some the end is a lingering, insidious one. Like all other animals, they are subject to parasitic attack, and parasitic wasps take a particularly heavy toll. With these creatures, the spider serves not as a meal for the adult, but as a living food supply for its developing offspring. An egg or eggs are laid in, or sometimes on, the body of a hapless spider which has been paralyzed by the wasp's sting. It is then buried underground, sometimes in a burrow dug by the wasp, or occasionally in one of its own making if it is a burrow-dwelling species. There the wasp larva feeds, develops, and grows at the expense of the gradually dwindling body of the spider.

Able to avoid the spider's deadly venom, a black-and-yellow mud-dauber wasp has immobilized a spider with its sting. Its fate is to become food for the wasp's developing larvae.

For many species such as the green lynx spider, parental care extends beyond the point where the eggs hatch. Although active, the spiderlings are still vulnerable to attack.

Camouflage and Mimicry

Many spiders have clearly decided that it is better to avoid detection in the first place than to have to defend themselves against attack. Whether in leaves, bark, twigs, flowers, or even bird droppings, if you search long and hard enough, there is likely to be a spider that either blends into or resembles its camouflage. Many of these examples of camouflage or mimicry serve a dual purpose, not only hiding the spider from potential predators but also concealing it from potential prey. A few examples of camouflage, usually accompanied by appropriate behavior, appear to have only a defensive function.

Many of the best examples are found among those tropical spiders which, as a matter of course, spend much of their lives resting on bark. These will generally have markings and coloration to suit a particular tree species and a flattened body fringed with hairs. These hairs serve an important function in that they reduce or almost eliminate any shadow that might be cast by the spider's legs and body.

The crab spiders (family Thomisidae) are a widespread group, so called for their crab-like, scuttling motion. There are numerous

The proportions of this elongate long-jawed orb-weaver, **Tetragnatha elongata,** *perfectly suit it when it needs to remain hidden on a plant stem.*

Living up to its name, the sand wolf spider, **Arctosa littoralis,** *blends in superbly with the sand grains on which it spends its time.*

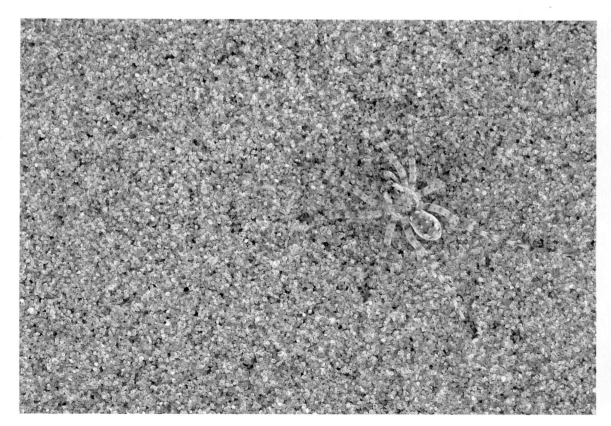

Lying pressed close to the bark of a tree, this huntsman or giant crab spider is superbly camouflaged. This enables it to avoid detection by predators and also to hide from potential prey.

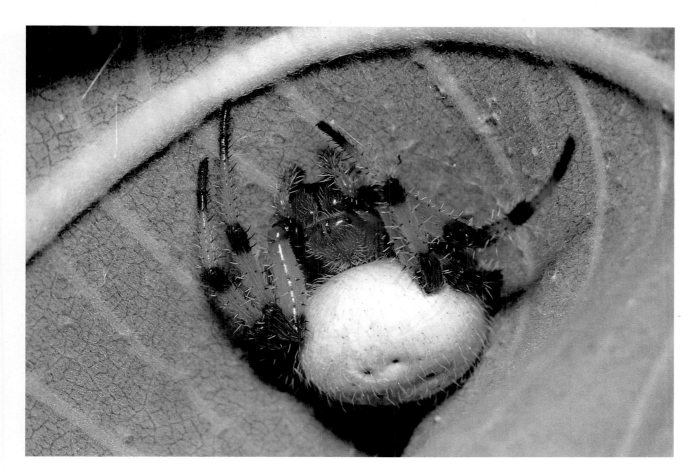

An orb-web spider, **Epeira raji**, lurks in the center of her nest, enshrouded by a leaf which she has incorporated into the structure.

With her body pressed close to its surface, a crab spider is protecting her egg sac from danger. Female spiders are renowned for the spirited defense which they will put up if danger threatens their developing offspring.

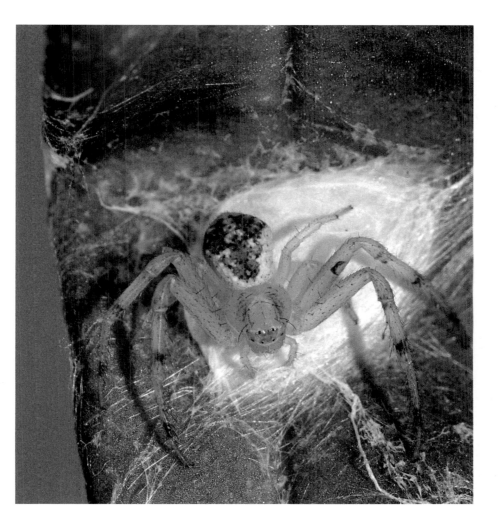

Following page: There can be few better examples of camouflage than that exhibited by this huntsman spider from southeast Asia. Its color and shape match the mossy background perfectly.

The green coloration of the green lynx spider affords it good camouflage as it guards its egg sac among the vegetation.

representatives in both Europe and North America, and their trademark is a wait-and-see approach to catching prey. Many species are colorful and rest among the petals of flowers. When they use their camouflage to good advantage, they are difficult to spot both by potential prey and by predators. When they choose the wrong color flower, however, they become an easy target.

The family Clubionidae contains representatives which are amazing mimics of ants. This mimicry extends not only to their appearance but also to their behavior—the spiders even appear to move like ants. One plausible explanation for this is that by mimicking ants, many potential predators are discouraged from attacking because of the vigor with which most ants defend themselves.

The spiky protrusions on the abdomen of an arrow-shaped micrathena spider, **Micrathena sagittata,** *presumably serve as a deterrent to would-be predatory birds.*

This ogre-faced or net-throwing spider, **Dinopis spinosa,** *is holding its web with its leg tips. When an insect passes by, the spider will quickly place the net over the victim, thus trapping it.*

Burrows, Tunnels, and Funnels

A popular means of concealment, especially among the large mygalomorph spiders, is to live in a burrow protected by a trapdoor which the inhabitant holds tightly shut if disturbed. It is from this protective hiding place that the spider makes furtive forays to catch passing prey, and into which it retreats if danger approaches. A trapdoor is fine when the threat posed is relatively small, but unfortunately serves little purpose against the wholesale digging up of burrow and spider. Both trap-door spiders and other types of spiders which live in tunnels without a trapdoor are subject to attacks from parasitic wasps.

Anyone who has ventured into a dank, dark cellar or the mouth of a cave will almost certainly have come across the large funnel-webs of spiders belonging to the family Agelenidae. At the center of the mesh of webbing lies a tubular retreat which usually extends into a crack or crevice. For much of the time the spider lurks just inside the entrance, ready to rush out if vibrations indicate prey has blundered onto the web. If the disturbance is more significant, then the spider retreats deep down the funnel tube.

A mygalomorph spider waits at the entrance to its silk-lined burrow for passing prey. Large insects will usually comprise the bulk of its diet.

Active Defense

For ground-dwelling spiders or those caught out in the open, the most obvious means of escaping from danger is to run away—a good strategy if you can move faster than your attacker. If threatened when clambering among vegetation, then a good ploy is to drop to the ground, either attached to a silk lifeline or not, depending on the species. A more robust attitude towards danger is adopted by some of the large bird-eating spiders, which arch their abdomens towards their attackers and then shake a cloud of irritating

hairs off the body and into the face of their foe; the hairs can set up a painful response in the skin and the membranes of the eyes, nose, and mouth.

An interesting method of escaping danger can be seen in the raft spider *Dolomedes fimbriatus*. Although this spider can reach a considerable size, with a legspan of up to 2 1/3 inches (6 centimeters), water-repellent hairs enable it to walk on water with impunity. If danger threatens, it can slide effortlessly through the surface film into the water below, thwarting the efforts of any terrestrial predator.

A wolf spider, **Pisaura mirabilis,** *lurks among the safety of the leaves among which it will disappear if danger threatens.*

Arachnophobia

Spiders are frequently found in mythology; among these tales is the Greek legend concerning Arachne, a maiden transformed into a spider for challenging a goddess in the art of spinning. She was condemned to a life spinning webs and gave her name to the Arachnids, the group to which spiders belong. Spiders' web-building skills feature in religion and folk legends from many other countries. Mohammed, for example, had his retreat concealed by a web-spinning spider, and the dogged determination of a spider to build a web inspired the Scottish hero Robert Bruce not to give up.

Many people have a mild fear and sometimes even a loathing of spiders, together with a healthy respect for them. But for a few, this antipathy takes the form of a pathological fear known as arachnophobia. Although strictly speaking, arachnophobia should include all members of the class Arachnida, there is little doubt that it is a specific fear of spiders with which it is commonly associated.

The speed with which spiders move and the sight of their often long, hairy legs can be off-putting, but a true fear of spiders is based on irrational feelings and cannot really be said to have a basis in fact. In Britain, for example, there are no spiders which are poisonous to man, although a few can deliver painful bites if provoked. Likewise, even in North America, where the infamous black widow lives, the incidence of spider-bite fatalities is trivially small by comparison with highway deaths—except, of course, to those few that actually get bitten. In actual fact, in terms of the numbers of insect pests they kill, spiders are greatly beneficial to all our lives.

In the past, our relationship with spiders might be said to have been more one of awe than of fear. It was, and still is in many countries, considered unlucky to kill a spider. Their industrious weaving skills have always been admired, although dust-filled webs are less welcome by the house-proud. Spiders' effectiveness in catching flies has, however, been greatly appreciated over the centuries.

Although reviled by some and revered by few, most people are able to tolerate the presence of spiders. By taking a closer look at the lifestyles and habits of spiders, a fascinating world is revealed. With such a range of species found literally on most doorsteps, the amateur naturalist does not have far to go to watch spiders, all of whom show fascinating adaptations to a predatory life in terms of both structure and behavior. Spend a few hours in the company of any spider, and curiosity or fear may turn to fascination and amazement at the skill of these industrious creatures.

Known in the Americas as a tarantula, this huge mygalomorph spider is a member of the family Theraphosidae. It lives in the Amazon rain forest and has here managed to catch and subdue a gecko.

Few creatures would be foolish enough to investigate these egg sacs which are being so jealously guarded by this female black widow spider, whose single bite can be fatal.

INDEX

*Page numbers in **bold-face** type indicate photo captions.*

Agelenidae, 68
anatomy of spiders, 7–12
  fangs, 20, **33**
  legs, **16**, 47–53
  sexual dimorphism and, 47
  skin, **30**
Arachne (mythical), 70
Arachnida, 7, 12
  origins of name, 70
arachophobia (fear of spiders), 70
Araneae, 12
Araneidae, 42
Araneomorpha (Labidognatha), 15–16
Argiope spiders, **7**, **44**
  Argiope trifasciata, **54**
Arthropods, 7
Australian black widow spider, **10**

baboon spiders
  king baboon spider (*Citharischius crawshayi*), **23**, **57**
  Usambara baboon spider, **15**, **20**
baby spiders (spiderlings)
  of Carolina wolf spiders (*Lycosa carolinensis*), **47**
  of green lynx spider (*Peucetia viridans*), **52**, **59**
  hatching of, 54
  of orb-web spiders, 54
banana spider, 12
behavior
  courtship and mating, 47–53
  egg-laying, 53–54
  hunting, 33–34
  mimicry, 66
  self-defense, 57
  sex differences and, 47
bird-eating spider (*Avicularia metallica*), **23**
bites by spiders, 23, 70
black-and-white Argiope spider, **7**
black-and-yellow Argiope spider (*Argiope aurantia*), **44**
black-and-yellow mud-dauber wasp, **59**
black widow spiders, 70
  Australian black widow spider, **10**
  egg sacs of, **70**
  Latrodectus mactans, **18**, **23**
  northern black widow spider (*Latrodectus variolus*), 7
bolas spiders (*Mastophora spp*), 41–42
Bruce, Robert, 70
burrowing wolf spider, **33**
burrows, 68, **68**

camouflage, 61–66
  by crab spider (*Misumena vatia*), **27**, **28**
  by giant crab spider (*Heteropoda venatoria*), **61**
  by green lynx spider (*Peucetia viridans*), **63**
  by huntsman spiders, **63**
  by wolf spider (*Pisaura mirabilis*), **69**
carapace, 10
Carolina wolf spider (*Lycosa carolinensis*), **47**
cephalothorax (prosoma), 7
chelicerae, 10, 15
chewing, **47**
classification of spiders, 12–16
Clubionidae, 66
Coleoptera (beetles), **58**
coloration of spiders, 5
  camouflage and mimicry in, 61–66, **61**, **69**
  of green lynx spider (*Peucetia viridans*), **63**
courtship of spiders, 47–53
crab spiders
  camouflage of, 61–66
  giant crab spider (*Heteropoda venatoria*), **30**, **61**
  Misumena vatia, **27**–30, **27**
  as prey for for beetles, **58**
  protection of egg sacs by, **63**

dark jumping spider (*Phidippus audax*), **34**, **35**
defensive behaviors, 57
  active, **69**
  camouflage and mimicry in, 61–66, **61**, **63**, **69**
  of egg sacs by female spiders, **63**
  fangs and venom for, 23
  by micrathena spider (*Micrathena sagittata*), **66**
digestive systems of spiders, 23

eggs, 53–54
  of Carolina wolf spiders (*Lycosa carolinensis*), **47**
egg sacs, 53–54
  of Argiope spiders, **54**
  of black widow spiders, **70**
  of crab spiders, **63**
  of green lynx spider (*Peucetia viridans*), **54**
  of nursery-web spider (*Pisaurina mira*), **52**
  of wolf spiders, **53**
eyes, 7
  of jumping spider (*Phidippus audax*), **35**
  of wolf spiders, **3**

fangs, 10, 20
  of burrowing wolf spider, **33**
feeding
  of animals on spiders, 57–58, **58**, **59**
  by baby spiders, 54
  by bird-eating spider (*Avicularia metallica*), **23**
  by black-and-yellow Argiope spider (*Argiope aurantia*), **44**
  chewing, **47**
  by crab spider (*Misumena vatia*), **27**, **27**, 30
  fangs and venom for, 20–23
  by grass spider, **15**, **41**, **42**
  by green lynx spider (*Peucetia viridans*), **23**
  hunting, 33–34
  by mygalomorph spiders, 20
  by neotropical wolf spider, **33**
  by shamrock spider (*Araneus trifolium*), **51**
  webs spun for, 44
  see also hunting
female spiders, 47
  baby spiders feeding on, 54
  egg-laying by, 53–54
  egg sacs protected by, **63**
  green lynx spider (*Peucetia viridans*), **54**
  wolf spiders, **53**
fishing spider (*Dolomedes triton*), **18**, **39**, **40**
funnel-shaped webs, 68
  of grass spider, **43**

giant crab spider (*Heteropoda venatoria*), **30**, **61**
giant nephilia spider, **11**
golden-silk (calico) spider (*Nephila clavipes*), **12**, **16**
grass spider, **15**, 41–**43**
green lynx spider (*Peucetia viridans*)
  camouflage of, **63**
  egg sacs guarded by, **54**
  hunting by, **23**
  spiderlings, **52**, **59**
growth and development of spiders, 10–12

house spiders, **23**
  bites from, 23
humans, 5
  fear of spiders (arachophobia) among, 70
  spider bites of, 23
hunting, 33–34
  by jumping spider (*Phidippus audax*), **34**, **35**
  traps set for, 41–42
  see also feeding
huntsman spiders, **63**

insects, 7, 42–44
  black-and-yellow mud-dauber wasp, **59**
  Coleoptera (beetles), **58**
  killed by spiders, 70
  mimicked by spiders, 66
  parasitic wasps, **58**, 68

jumping spider (*Phidippus audax*), **7**, **33**, **34**, **35**

king baboon spider (*Citharischius crawshayi*), **23**, **57**

Labidognatha (Araneomorpha), 15–16
legs, 10, **16**
  used in courtship, 47–53
Linyphid spiders, 44
long-jawed orb-weaver spider (*Tetragnatha elongata*), **61**

mabel orchard spider (*Leucauge mabelae*), **5**
male spiders, 47–53
mating of spiders, 47–53
micrathena spider (*Micrathena sagittata*), **66**
mimicry by spiders, 66
Mohammed, 70
molting, 10–12, 15
  by fishing spider, **18**
mouths, 10
mygalomorph spiders (Orthognatha), 15
  burrows of, 68, **68**
  feeding by, 20, **20**
  tarantulas, 70
mythology, spiders in, 70

neotropical orb-weaver spider, **57**
neotropical wolf spider, **33**
net-throwing (ogre-faced) spider (*Dinlopis spinosa*), **66**
northern black widow spider (*Latrodectus variolus*), 7
nursery-web spider (*Pisaurina mira*), **52**

ogre-faced (net-throwing) spider (*Dinlopis spinosa*), **66**
orb-weaver spiders, 42–44, **51**
  Epeira raji, **11**, **63**
  long-jawed orb-weaver spider (*Tetragnatha elongata*), **61**
  neotropical orb-weaver spider, **57**
  silk produced by, 18
  spiderlings, 54

Orthognatha, *see* mygalomorph spiders

parasitic wasps, **58**, 68
pedipalps, 10
pheromones, 47
prosoma (cephalothorax), 7, 10
purse-web spider (*Atypus affinis*), 41

raft spiders (*Dolomedes sp*), 20, 33–34
  (*Dolomedes fimbriatus*), **69**
reproduction
  eggs in, 53–54
  sex differences and, 47

St. Andrew's cross spider, **17**
sand wolf spider (*Arctosa littoralis*), **61**
self-defense, 57
  see also defensive behaviors
sense organs, 7–10
sex differences among spiders, 47
shamrock spider (*Araneus trifolium*), **51**
silk, 5, 16–18, **18**, **44**
  non-web uses of, 41–42
  used in reproduction, 53
  webs spun from, 44
  see also webs
six-spotted fishing spider (*Dolomedes triton*), **39**, **40**
skin of spiders, **30**
slit organs, 10
species of spiders, 12
spiderlings, *see* baby spiders
spiders
  active defense by, **69**
  anatomy of, 7–10
  burrows and tunnels of, 68, **68**
  camouflage and mimicry in coloration of, 61–66, **61**, **63**, **69**
  classification of, 12–16
  courtship and mating of, 47–53
  egg-laying by, 53–54
  fangs and venom of, 20–23
  fear of (arachophobia), 70
  growth and development of, 10–12
  hunting by, 33–34
  self-defense by, 57
  sex differences among, 47
  threats to, 57–58, **58**, **59**
spiny orb-weaver spider (*Gasteracantha elipsoides*), **51**
spitting spider (*Scytodes thoracica*), 41
Sydney funnel-web spider (*Atrax robustus*), **23**

tarantulas, 70
Theraphosidae, 70
touch, sense of, 7–10
trap-door spiders, 41, 68
tunnels, 68

Usambara baboon spider, **15**, **20**

venom, 20–23
  of black widow spiders, **10**
  of crab spider (*Misumena vatia*), **28**
  of neotropical orb-weaver spider, **57**
vision, in spiders, 33

wasps, **58**, 68
water spider, 34
webs, 5, 16–18, **17**, **18**
  of black-and-yellow Argiope spider (*Argiope aurantia*), **44**
  classifying spiders by, 15
  funnel-shaped, **43**, 68
  of giant nephilia spider, **11**
  of golden-silk (calico) spider (*Nephila clavipes*), **16**
  of ogre-faced (net-throwing) spider (*Dinlopis spinosa*), **66**
  orb-webs, 42–44
  of St. Andrew's cross spider, **17**
  of water spider, **34**
wolf spiders, **3**, 33, **35**
  burrowing wolf spider, **33**
  Carolina wolf spider (*Lycosa carolinensis*), **47**
  egg sacs of, 53, **53**–54
  neotropical wolf spider, **33**
  Pisaura mirabilis, **69**
  sand wolf spider (*Arctosa littoralis*), **61**

young spiders, *see* baby spiders

zebra spider (*Salticus scenicus*), **33**